Picture Stories

Order the pictures from first to last.

Use Tiles ❶, ❷, ❸, ❹.

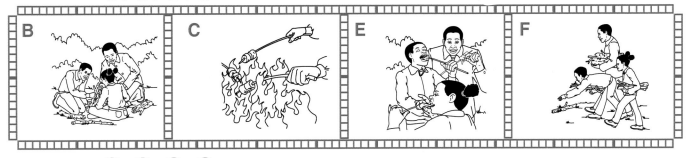

Use Tiles ❺, ❻, ❼, ❽.

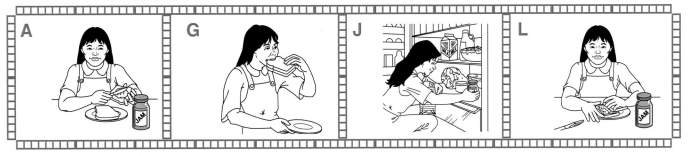

Use Tiles ❾, ❿, ⓫, ⓬.

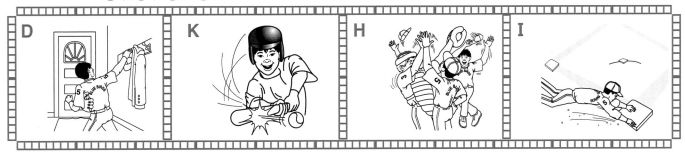

Be sure to look at all four pictures first. Then put them in order.

Objective: Place events in sequential order; practice comprehension skills.

1

Mixed-Up Paragraphs

Order the sentences so that the paragraphs make sense.

Use Tiles ❶, ❷, ❸, ❹, ❺, ❻.

A   The starter blew the whistle and dropped the flag.

D   The runners lined up at the starting line.

F   It was the day of the big race.

C   The crowd cheered as the winner crossed the finish line.

E   The runners darted off the starting line.

G   Each runner ran as quickly as she could.

Use Tiles ❼, ❽, ❾, ❿, ⓫, ⓬.

B   Next, they sorted the building blocks into matching piles.

I   Finally, they pretended they were defending the king.

K   Rick, Jeff, and Lucia decided to make a castle out of building blocks.

H   When the castle was finished, they added the knights with swords and shields.

L   They began building the walls of the castle.

J   First, they looked over the directions.

> Be sure to read all the sentences first. Remember, the first sentence should tell about all the other sentences.

Objective: Arrange sentences in a logical sequential order in paragraphs; practice comprehension skills.

Paragraph Puzzles

Order the sentences so that the paragraphs make sense.

Use Tiles ❶ , ❷ , ❸ , ❹ , ❺ , ❻ .

F   It didn't take long after the phone call for the fire trucks to arrive.

G   The firefighters quickly put out the fire.

I   Jon's mother dialed 9–1–1 for help.

K   Then they ran next door to use the phone.

J   Jon saw flames coming out of the oven.

H   Instead of panicking, he quickly shouted for his mother.

> Remember, the first sentence of a paragraph usually tells what the rest of the paragraph is about.

Use Tiles ❼ , ❽ , ❾ , ❿ , ⓫ , ⓬ .

C   When they returned home, they decorated the house.

B   When everything was ready, Kendra heard the doorbell ring. Her friends had arrived!

E   The last thing they did was frost the cake.

D   Kendra's mom gave her permission to have a party.

L   After she sent out the invitations, she and her father bought decorations.

A   She sent out her party invitations.

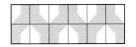

Objective: Arrange sentences in a logical sequential order in paragraphs; practice comprehension and writing process skills.

3

Putting Paragraphs Together

**Find the sentences that relate to each topic.
Order the sentences so that they make sense.**

Remember, the sentences in a paragraph are all about the same topic. The order of the sentences needs to make sense.

Paragraph 1

Find and place in order **three** sentences about a **party**.

1 ◼

2 ◼

3 ◼

Paragraph 2

Find and place in order **four** sentences about a **magician and the last trick he performs**.

4 ◼

5 ◼

6 ◼

7 ◼

Paragraph 3

Find and place in order **five** sentences about the **last seconds of a football game**.

8 ▢

9 ▢

10 ▢

11 ▢

12 ▢

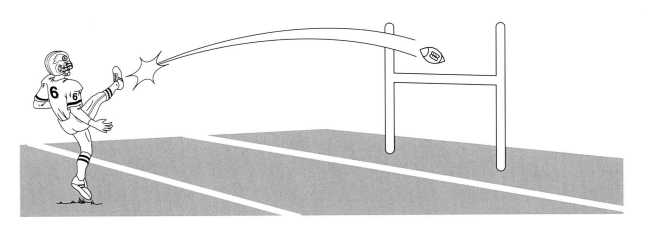

Answer Box ···

A	B	C	D	E	F
The home team won the game!	They watched from the window as Tina drove up with her father.	The audience cheered in amazement.	The kicker came on the field to attempt the field goal.	He said the magic words, "Hocus Pocus."	The visitors' defense stopped the touchdown.
G	**H**	**I**	**J**	**K**	**L**
Then he reached in and pulled a rabbit out of his hat.	The home team ran the ball down the field.	The guests arrived early at Tina's house.	For his grand finale, the magician waved his wand over his black hat.	When Tina walked in the door, they all yelled, "Surprise!"	He kicked the ball through the goal posts.

Objective: Classify sentences according to topic; arrange sentences in a logical sequential order; practice writing process skills.

5

Put Story Events in Order

Read the story. Think about the order in which things happen.

The Panda and the Koala

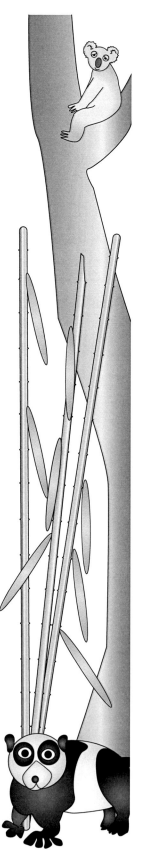

Once upon a time, a wise tiger ruled over the jungle animals. All the other animals respected him because he was fair and kept peace in the jungle. Whenever the animals had a problem, they would go to the tiger for advice.

One day the panda and the koala met with the wise tiger. They were fighting over the delicious yellow jungle flowers. They were a special treat and both animals wanted all the flowers to themselves. The tiger thought it over and decided that the panda and koala should share. There were enough flowers for them both. The koala and panda reluctantly agreed.

The next day, the tiger was walking through the jungle and saw the panda and koala fighting again. The tiger wanted peace in the jungle. He had had enough of the two selfish animals. He gave the panda and koala one more chance to share, and they refused. He decided that the selfish animals should leave the jungle and the yellow flowers. He ordered the panda to move to China and eat bamboo plants. He ordered the koala to move to Australia and eat eucalyptus leaves. You can still find the animals in those countries today, wishing they had the delicious yellow flowers!

Order the events as they happened in the story.
Use Tiles ❶, ❷, ❸, ❹, ❺, ❻.

C   The tiger decided that he was tired of selfish behavior.

G   The panda and the koala were fighting over the flowers again.

H   The koala and the panda went to the tiger for advice.

I   The panda and koala reluctantly agreed to share.

K   The wise tiger said that there were enough flowers for both animals to share.

L   The tiger sent the panda to China.

Read the story. Think about the order of events.

The Spelling Bee

Benito could not wait for school to start. He was going to a brand new school for sixth grade. On the very first day, his teacher, Ms. Turley, announced a spelling bee was going to take place in three weeks. Only three weeks! Benito would have to study hard to do well in the contest.

He took the spelling list home and studied hard every day. Benito's mother helped him after school, his father helped him after work, and his grandpa helped him on Saturdays. He studied hard at school, too. Ms. Turley even held special practice sessions. The winners of the school spelling bee would go on to the city finals. Benito lived and breathed spelling words for the whole three weeks!

The night before the contest, Benito could hardly sleep. He knew many other students who had been working as hard as he. He was worried. Had he studied enough? Would Ms. Turley give him a word that he did not know how to spell?

At last, the big moment arrived. All of Benito's family watched as Benito spelled word after word. When it came down to the last word, Benito and Kelly were the last two students. Even though Kelly ended up winning the spelling bee, Benito was proud. He came in second in a brand-new school, and Ms. Turley said he could enter the city contest!

Order the events as they happened in the story.
Use Tiles 7, 8, 9, 10, 11, 12.

A Benito could hardly sleep the night before the contest.

B Benito started a new school.

D Kelly won the spelling bee.

E Ms. Turley asked Benito to enter the city contest.

F Ms. Turley announced a spelling bee in three weeks.

J Benito studied hard at home and at school.

Objective: Read a story and arrange events from it in chronological order; practice comprehension skills.

7

Once Upon a Time

Read each list of characters. Find the type of book in which you are most likely to meet these characters.

1 a talking mouse, a lion that sews clothes

2 George Washington, Martha Washington

3 a third grade teacher, her students

4 an explorer, a team of sled dogs

5 a detective, suspects

6 Paul Bunyan, Pecos Bill

Think about books you have read. Ask yourself, "Where have I seen these characters before?"

Read each book title. Find the characters that are most likely to appear in the book.

7 *Important Moments in American History*

8 *There's a What in the Castle?*

9 *Across the Great Plains*

10 *The Case of the Missing Watch*

11 *Tori's Science Fair Disaster!*

12 *Dinosaur Dig*

 **Answer Box** •

A	B	C	D	E	F
Abraham Lincoln and Betsy Ross	fantasy story	biography	tall tale	realistic story	a fifth-grade girl and her classmates
G	**H**	**I**	**J**	**K**	**L**
adventure story	Detective Brown and Jake the bloodhound	Princess Penelope and her pet dragon	a paleontologist and his team	mystery story	pioneers heading West

Objective: Analyze, classify, and make inferences about characters in books; practice comprehension skills.

Mathematically Speaking

Read each group of words. Find the best title for the group.

1 triangle, square, circle, rectangle

2 two, four, six, eight, ten

3 inch, foot, yard

4 ounce, pound, ton

5 54, 86, 72, 61

6 5, 10, 15, 20

Read each title. Find a member of that group.

7 shapes

8 even numbers

9 units of distance measurement

10 numbers less than 50

11 units of weight measurement

12 multiples of 5

Answer Box

A	B	C	D	E	F
mile	numbers greater than 50	shapes	oval	even numbers	95
G	H	I	J	K	L
gram	units of distance	43	units of weight	58	multiples of 5

Objective: Classify mathematical terms;
practice comprehension and vocabulary skills.

9

In a Class of Their Own

Read each group of words. Find the best title for the group.

1 California, Utah, Illinois, New York, Texas

2 New York City, Dallas, Sacramento, Miami

3 Apache, Navajo, Sioux, Mohawk, Hopi

4 Grand Tetons, Everglades, Grand Canyon, Yosemite, Yellowstone

5 Atlantic, Pacific, Indian

6 George Washington, Abraham Lincoln, William Clinton

7 flag, Liberty Bell, Statue of Liberty, bald eagle

8 Africa, South America, North America, Europe

9 July, September, November, February

10 Monday, Saturday, Thursday, Wednesday

11 mountain, peninsula, atoll

12 Mississippi River, Gulf of Mexico, Red Sea

We're in the overalls group!

Answer Box

A	B	C	D	E	F
cities	U.S. Presidents	months	Native American peoples	United States National Parks	states

G	H	I	J	K	L
bodies of water	continents	land forms	oceans	days of the week	U.S. symbols

Objective: Categorize social studies terms; practice comprehension and vocabulary skills.

Scientifically Speaking

Read each group of words.
Find the best title for the group.

1 sparrow, eagle, hawk

2 Neptune, Saturn, Venus

3 bee, butterfly, ant

4 bear, dog, human

5 rose, daisy, carnation

6 oak, pine, apple

Read each title.
Find a member of that group.

7 insects

8 flowers

9 birds

10 trees

11 reptiles

12 planets

Fig. 12

Alaskan Brown Bear *Ursus middendorfii* This bear is the largest flesh-eating land mammal. It is closely related to the Gr... ...likes to steal... ...kets.

Think about how all the words on the list are alike before you choose the title.

Answer Box

A	B	C	D	E	F
insects	crow	trees	planets	birds	mammals
G	H	I	J	K	L
crocodile	flowers	Mars	tulip	beetle	maple

Picture This!

Zoe, the zoologist, is studying six beautiful butterflies. Find the butterfly that matches each description.

1. Daisy the butterfly has ten small spots on each wing.

2. Harry the butterfly has six spots on one wing and seven on the other.

3. Bernice the butterfly has bent antennae and two spots on each wing.

4. Jaime the butterfly has curly antennae and four spots on each wing.

5. Margo the butterfly has stripes on her wings and is wearing boots.

6. Bobby the butterfly has zig-zag antennae and stripes on his wings.

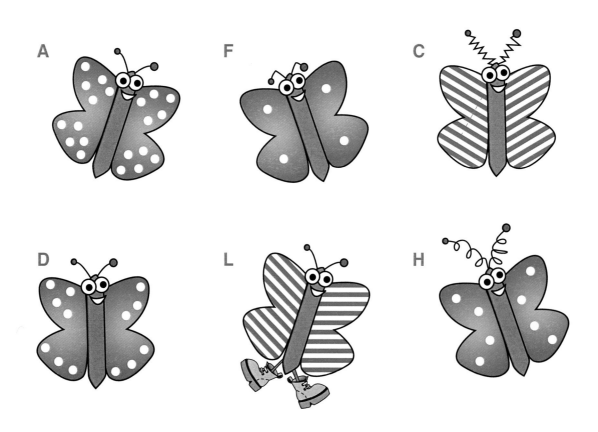

Troy is choosing a bicycle for his birthday!
Find the bike that matches each description.

7 This bike has three wheels.

8 This bike has a water bottle and streamers on the handle bars.

9 This bike has a horn.

10 This bike has a basket on the front.

11 Troy found a bike with his name on the license plate.

12 This bike has a flag.

Precise descriptions will make your own writing more interesting for your readers.

I

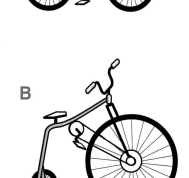

E

K

B

J

G

Objective: Read precise descriptions to match phrases with illustrations; practice comprehension, writing, and study skills.

13

Take Note!

Read the following notes. Think about the information in each note.

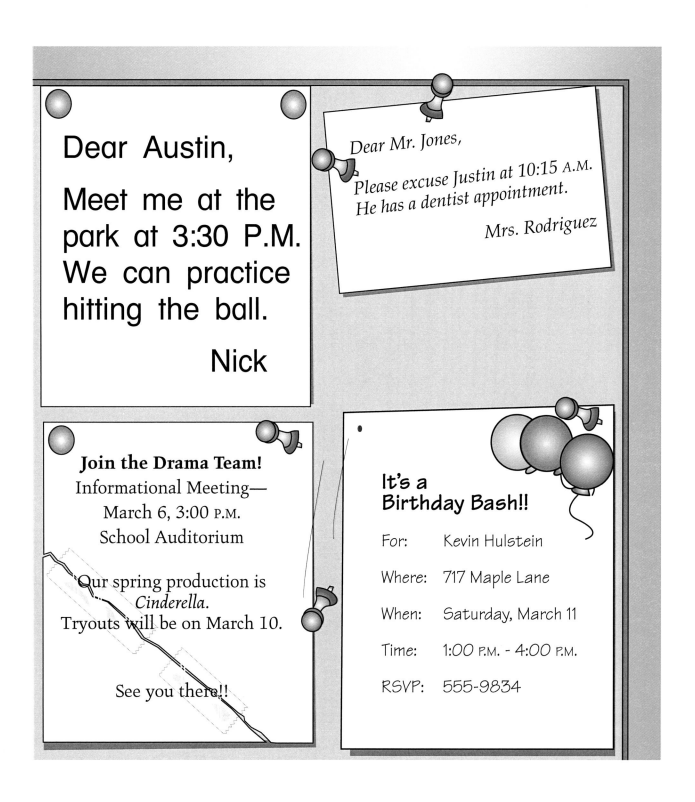

Dear Austin,

Meet me at the park at 3:30 P.M. We can practice hitting the ball.

Nick

Dear Mr. Jones,

Please excuse Justin at 10:15 A.M. He has a dentist appointment.

Mrs. Rodriguez

Join the Drama Team!
Informational Meeting—
March 6, 3:00 P.M.
School Auditorium

Our spring production is
Cinderella.
Tryouts will be on March 10.

See you there!!

It's a
Birthday Bash!!

For: Kevin Hulstein

Where: 717 Maple Lane

When: Saturday, March 11

Time: 1:00 P.M. - 4:00 P.M.

RSVP: 555-9834

Now use the notes to answer the following questions.

1 Whom will Nick meet at the park?

2 Where does Justin need to go at 10:15 A.M.?

3 When is the drama team meeting?

4 What kind of party is Kevin having?

5 Why is Austin meeting Nick?

6 What is the spring production?

7 Kevin's birthday party is on ▮.

8 ▮ wrote Justin's note.

9 Kevin's party ends at ▮.

10 The meeting on March 6 is in ▮.

11 Kevin lives at ▮.

12 ▮ are being held on March 10.

Remember,
answer the
questions who,
what, when,
where, and why
in notes of your
own.

Answer Box

A	B	C	D	E	F
Austin	birthday party	4:00 P.M.	March 6	the dentist	*Cinderella*

G	H	I	J	K	L
the school auditorium	March 11	717 Maple Lane	to practice hitting	Mrs. Rodriguez	tryouts

Objective: Read to locate information; extract relevant details from a text;
practice comprehension and study skills.

Planet Facts

Read the passage. Look for facts about planets.

In the last few years, astronomers have learned a lot about the planets Mercury, Venus, and Mars. Special spacecrafts equipped with cameras have flown near each planet to take pictures of the planets' surfaces. From these pictures, scientists have been able to draw very detailed maps of each planet's surface. Spacecrafts have even taken samples of Mars's soil and Venus's atmosphere. What have we learned from these samples? One thing the samples have shown is that life as we know it on Earth cannot exist on these planets.

Mercury, the closest planet to the sun, takes about 88 "Earth days" to revolve around the sun and about 59 "Earth days" to rotate on its axis. This means that its day is almost as long as its year. Mercury's surface is covered with cracks and craters. We could not live on Mercury. There is no air to breathe. The side of Mercury that faces the sun would be too hot for us, and the side away from the sun would be too cold.

Venus, the second planet from the sun, is sometimes called Earth's twin—this is because Earth and Venus are about the same size. The size is the only way in which they are the same. On Venus, the air is poisonous gas, the wind is stronger than a hurricane, the surface is hot enough to melt lead, and the sun rises in the west. Venus takes 225 "Earth days" to go around the sun and 243 "Earth days" to rotate on its axis. This means that, on Venus, a day is longer than a year!

Mars is the fourth planet away from the sun. Mars has many of the same natural features of Earth, such as volcanoes and canyons. Mars also has two small moons. Its surface is red, even when seen from Earth. It takes Mars 687 "Earth days" to revolve around the sun. It takes about 24 hours for Mars to revolve on its axis, so days on Mars are about the same length as days on Earth.

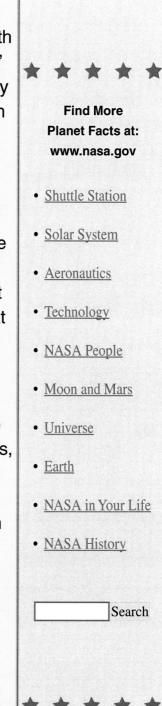

★ ★ ★ ★ ★

**Find More
Planet Facts at:
www.nasa.gov**

- Shuttle Station

- Solar System

- Aeronautics

- Technology

- NASA People

- Moon and Mars

- Universe

- Earth

- NASA in Your Life

- NASA History

Search

★ ★ ★ ★ ★

Dr. Samuel is an astronomer who is observing the planets.
Use the information in the article to complete his field notes.

Monday, May 4

1 ▪ , the closest planet to the sun, is covered with **2** ▪ , so it looks like a raisin! With my telescope, I zeroed in on **3** ▪ , a planet that is similar to Earth in size. The other planet I observed was Mars, the **4** ▪ planet from the sun. It has a surface different from Earth's—it looks **5** ▪ . But Mars and Earth are alike in some ways. They both have **6** ▪ .

Wednesday, May 6

I took these notes using information from **7** ▪ that have traveled to the planets. The samples show that we **8** ▪ live on these other planets. Spacecrafts **9** ▪ get samples from these planets for scientists to study. We have found that the air on Venus is **10** ▪ . On Venus, a day is **11** ▪ than a year. A day on **12** ▪ is about as long as a day on Earth.

Answer Box

A	B	C	D	E	F
fourth	poisonous	cracks and craters	Mars	Venus	longer

G	H	I	J	K	L
spacecrafts	Mercury	cannot	volcanoes and canyons	red	can

Objective: Read nonfiction text to gain information; complete sentences with details from the text; practice comprehension skills.

17

What's Missing?

Read each paragraph. Find the sentence that should be placed into each paragraph.

1   Mary's favorite sport is soccer. She practices at home with her brothers. She also practices three times a week with her teammates. This year, her team made the playoffs.

2   Every day after school, James walks Mr. Manfrey's dog. He enjoys playing with the dog and he gets five dollars a week. Mr. Manfrey thinks that James does a great job!

3   Dave really likes music. He plays the guitar in a band with his friends. He also plays the violin in the school orchestra. When he isn't playing music, he is listening to it.

4   Mr. Stevens, our principal, likes September. It marks the start of fall, his favorite season. Mr. Stevens enjoys football games and cool weather. Most of all, he loves the beginning of a new school year.

5   February is my favorite month. We have a Valentine's Day party at school. We also get two school days off to celebrate Presidents' birthdays. Best of all, February is a short month, so my allowance doesn't have to last as long!

6   Maria is a good student. She studies hard. She listens well in class and asks questions when she doesn't understand something. Maria has a special place at home where she does her homework every night.

7   Jenna was selected to be the treasurer of her class. Math is easy for her, so her classmates decided that she would be a good person to keep track of the money.

8   You might call Craig a "sports nut!" He enjoys many different sports. He is a good quarterback. He is a starter on the school basketball team and a pitcher for the school baseball team.

9   Jillian enjoys walking on the beach. At sunrise, the beach is quiet. It is a good chance for Jillian to think about things. The sunlight looks beautiful on the waves, too.

10   Rick is very tall. His grandfather is also tall. Every year, Grandpa measures Rick to see if he has grown.

11   Nikki has been saving her money for six months. Last week, she bought a bike with her money. She learned the reward of saving money a little bit at a time.

12   Kris has a friend named Ben. They are in the same class at school, and they spend time together after school, too. They ride bikes, swim, and fish together.

Answer Box

A	B	C	D	E	F
Now he is looking for more pets to walk.	She follows directions and completes her work on time.	Sometimes she invites her father to walk with her so they can talk.	He takes piano lessons.	She knows that practicing will make her a better player.	He always looks forward to September.
G	**H**	**I**	**J**	**K**	**L**
They sit by each other at lunch every day.	In the summer, he is on the swim team.	My birthday is on February 8.	She worked hard to earn her money by doing chores.	She felt proud to be elected and promised to do a good job.	He is the tallest boy in the class.

Objective: Determine the topic of a paragraph and the details that support it; practice comprehension and writing process skills.

19

Tell Me a Riddle

Read the riddles. Find the word that solves each riddle.

1 I can light up a room. I'm very bright, even though I wear a shade.

2 I am very independent. You celebrate me with fireworks.

3 I'm "man's best friend," even if I do have to fetch things for him.

4 They say you can't tell me by my cover. But look between my covers and you can tell a lot.

5 I have a trunk though I'm not going on a trip.

6 You might have me in your throat or find me on a lily pad.

7 The sharper I am, the shorter I get. I can draw a straight line or write a letter.

8 Clumsy people say they are all me. If you're good at growing things, people might say that you have one of me that is green.

9 Tables have four of me. People have two of me. I'm something you stand on.

10 You put me on one leg at a time.

11 You look through me to see outside. I'm a real "pane."

12 I shine all day. I'm the brightest star. I'm really hot!

Remember, some riddles are puns! Puns have words with two meanings that are used in a funny way.

Answer Box

A	B	C	D	E	F
window	elephant	book	lamp	sun	thumb
G	H	I	J	K	L
dog	leg	pencil	pants	Fourth of July	frog

Objective: Make inferences to solve riddles; practice comprehension skills.

Tell Me Another Riddle

Read the riddles. Find the word that solves each riddle.

1 I'm all through your house. There are many kinds of me, including screen, front, and back.

2 Five, six, pick up "me." I'm great for starting a campfire and for playing a drum.

3 Everyone on the beach wears me. You might call me "shades."

4 I ran up a clock. I love cheese. I move the cursor on your computer.

5 You can drink my juice. I'm in a rainbow or on a tree.

6 I sound like "rows," and I smell sweet. I am beautiful, but be careful when you pick me.

7 I am a kind of flower. I'm also the color purple.

8 I can hold your spare change or keep your hand warm.

9 I go around town. I'm worthless when I'm flat. When I'm at my best, I'm full of air.

10 I'm how sad people feel. I'm a berry and a bird.

11 Sometimes you push me to get on an elevator.

12 I peck the ground. I wake the farmer each morning.

 Answer Box ···

A	B	C	D	E	F
button	orange	rose	sticks	blue	violet
G	**H**	**I**	**J**	**K**	**L**
tire	sunglasses	pocket	rooster	door	mouse

Get the Message!

Read the notices on the Community Bulletin Board. Think about the *who, what, when, where,* and *why* in each notice.

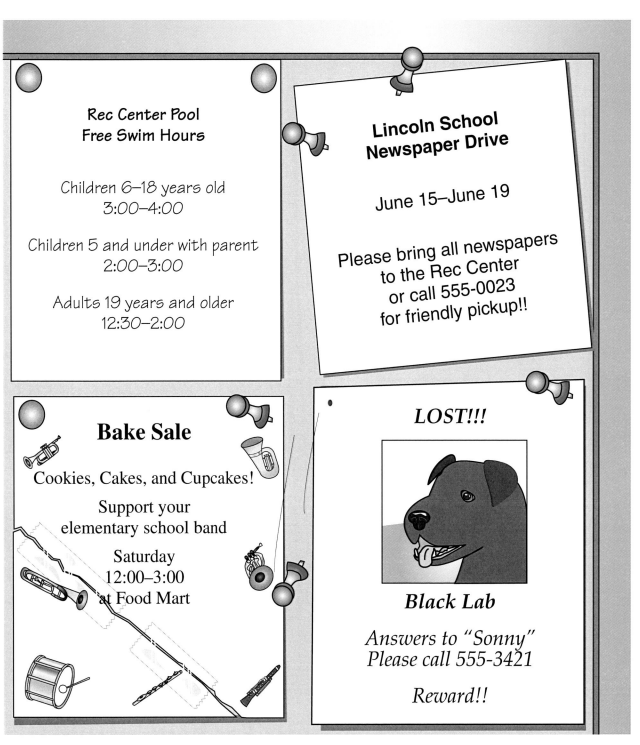

Rec Center Pool
Free Swim Hours

Children 6–18 years old
3:00–4:00

Children 5 and under with parent
2:00–3:00

Adults 19 years and older
12:30–2:00

Lincoln School Newspaper Drive

June 15–June 19

Please bring all newspapers to the Rec Center or call 555-0023 for friendly pickup!!

Bake Sale

Cookies, Cakes, and Cupcakes!

Support your elementary school band

Saturday
12:00–3:00
at Food Mart

LOST!!!

Black Lab

*Answers to "Sonny"
Please call 555-3421*

Reward!!

Use the information in the notices to answer the questions.

1 You found a black Lab puppy. What should you do?

2 Your three-year-old brother wants to swim. When can he go?

3 How can you help out at Lincoln School?

4 The elementary school band needs a new drum. What can you do?

5 You want to take your friends swimming for your party. Where can you go?

6 What is the name of the lost black Lab?

7 Where do you go to support the school band?

8 When is the newspaper drive?

9 When can a group of 10-year-olds swim for free?

10 When is the band's bake sale?

11 Where can you drop off your newspapers?

12 What will you get if you find the black Lab?

Remember, include specific details when you write announcements or notices of your own.

A	B	C	D	E	F
a reward	June 15–19	Food Mart	Saturday 12:00–3:00	Rec Center Pool	Rec Center

G	H	I	J	K	L
Sonny	from 2:00–3:00	buy some cookies	Call 555-3421	donate newspapers	from 3:00–4:00

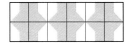

Objective: Identify relevant details in informational writing; practice comprehension skills.

23

Find the Topic Sentence

Read the paragraphs. Find the best topic sentence for each paragraph.

1   Cirrus clouds are wispy. Stratus clouds are layers of flat clouds. Cumulus clouds are tall piles of white clouds. Nimbus clouds are dark rain clouds.

2   Dark clouds filled the sky and thunder boomed in the distance. Soon the rain would be falling and puddles would be forming.

3   They laid in the grass, looking up. They pretended the clouds were circus trains, dragons, and race cars.

4   Max watched as the large trucks pulled into town. Soon the tents would be up. Max couldn't wait to see the elephants, tigers, and other circus animals.

5   Max loved the sight of the tents. He loved the silly clowns and the taste of cotton candy. He couldn't wait to hear the ringmaster calling everyone to their seats.

A topic sentence gives the main idea of a paragraph. A topic sentence could be the first or last sentence.

6   Molten rock from below the earth's surface forms gas and builds up pressure, causing a volcano to explode. Some eruptions cause clouds of gas, dust, rocks, and lava to explode high into the air. Other eruptions release a gentle flow of lava.

7   Igneous rock is made from hot liquid that cools. Sedimentary rock is made from material deposited by wind, water, and glaciers. Metamorphic rock is created by heat and pressure.

⑧ It works by receiving messages from the nerves. Everything you learn is kept here. Your brain does your thinking and feeling. It tells your muscles when to move.

⑨ The brain serves as the main control center of your body. The spinal cord carries messages between your brain and the other parts of your body. The nerves send the messages from your skin and sense organs to the brain.

⑩ Each of them takes information from the outside of your body and sends it to the brain. Your eyes see, your skin feels, your nose smells, your ears hear, and your mouth tastes.

⑪ The word continent means "self-contained." Asia, Africa, Antarctica, North America, South America, Australia, and Europe are continents. Except for Europe and Asia, most of the continents are surrounded, or nearly surrounded, by water.

⑫ Cartographers make maps of different places. Some make maps of the stars and space. Other cartographers make maps of the ocean floor, the world, or of cities and states. A cartographer must be very accurate when making a map.

Answer Box

A	B	C	D	E	F
There are four types of clouds.	The circus was coming.	The children enjoyed watching the cumulus clouds float by.	Earth has seven continents.	A storm was coming.	A volcano is a special type of mountain that erupts.

G	H	I	J	K	L
The sense organs are the eyes, nose, mouth, ears, and skin.	There are three types of rock.	Max loved the circus.	Your nervous system is made up of the brain, spinal cord, nerves, and sense organs.	Your brain serves as the main control center of your body.	A person who makes maps is called a cartographer.

Objective: Identify the topic sentence (main idea) of a paragraph; practice comprehension and writing process skills.

25

Details, Details

Read the paragraphs. Find the main idea for each paragraph.

1   Mt. Everest is a very tall mountain in the Himalayan Mountain range. It is 29,028 feet, or nearly five and one-half miles, high—making it taller than any other mountain.

2   The hummingbird is the smallest bird in the world. It can fly up, down, backward, forward, sideways, and even upside down. As it flies, its wings vibrate to make a humming sound.

3   Birds migrate to find sunlight, food, or warmer temperatures. Birds don't "think" about when to go—they follow their instincts. Some birds migrate up to 1,800 miles.

4   The oxygen in the air we breathe comes from plants. Plants also provide many of the foods we eat, including grains, fruits, vegetables, and spices. Paper, rubber, and wood also come from plants.

5   Roots take in water and minerals from the ground. The stem provides stability for the plant and contains cells that carry the water and minerals to the leaves. The leaves release gases into the air.

> When you write, think of what you want your readers to remember. Write sentences to support that idea.

6   Chlorophyll is found in green plants. Using energy from the sun, chlorophyll combines with a gas in the air and water to make sugars and starches. These sugars and starches are stored as food for the plant.

7   The Ring of Fire is a loop of volcanoes circling the Pacific Ocean. More than half of the 400 known volcanoes on Earth form this ring of fire. Volcanoes in the Ring of Fire erupt often.

8   The Arctic region surrounds the North Pole and the Antarctic region is at the South Pole. The Arctic region has polar bears and the Antarctic region has penguins. The Arctic region has total sunlight when the Antarctic region has total darkness. Then they reverse, leaving the Arctic dark and the Antarctic light.

26

⑨ The largest iceberg in the Northern Hemisphere was recorded at eight miles long and almost four miles wide, with a weight of over nine billion tons. Some icebergs jut hundreds of feet out of the water and look like huge ice mountains.

⑩ Geysers form from water that seeps into the ground and then is heated by the magma beneath Earth's surface. As the water heats up, the water begins to boil and turns to steam. This steam builds up pressure until it bursts out of the ground.

⑪ Yellowstone National Park is the home to over 200 geysers. People from all over the world come to see the geyser Old Faithful. It spurts water up to 130 feet high every 33 to 120 minutes. It has been blowing off steam on schedule for more than 100 years.

⑫ The Grand Canyon is home to the Colorado River. The Colorado River runs for 277 miles at the bottom of the mile-deep canyon.

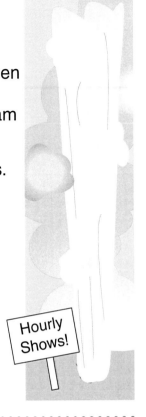

Hourly Shows!

Answer Box

A	B	C	D	E	F
It is the tallest mountain in the world.	People need plants for many reasons.	The Antarctic and the Arctic regions are different in several ways.	This fast-moving river has helped to shape the Grand Canyon.	Icebergs are chunks of frozen ice.	Migration is the seasonal movement of birds.
G	**H**	**I**	**J**	**K**	**L**
Geysers are hot springs that allow water and steam to escape from Earth.	Most of the world's active volcanoes are found in the Pacific Ocean.	The hummingbird is a very unique bird.	Plants are able to make their own food.	Old Faithful is one of the most famous geysers in the world.	Plants have roots, a stem, and leaves.

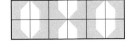

Objective: Identify the main idea of a paragraph and the details that support it; practice comprehension and writing process skills.

27

What's the Big Idea?

Read the paragraphs. Then find the best topic sentence for each paragraph.

1   Scientists believe that it weighed 8 tons, measured about 25 feet in length, and stood $9\frac{1}{2}$ feet tall. About one-third of its size was its enormous head and large horns. It was probably a good fighter.

2   It grows to about 100 feet long and can weigh over 150 tons. This is about 25 times larger than an adult African elephant. The blue whale can eat about 4 tons of shrimp a day.

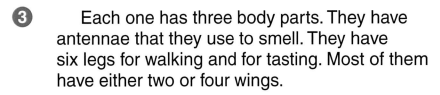

Remember, the topic sentence tells what the rest of the sentences are about.

3   Each one has three body parts. They have antennae that they use to smell. They have six legs for walking and for tasting. Most of them have either two or four wings.

4   Some scientists believe that this large creature chased down other dinosaurs and ate them. Its name means "Tyrant Lizard King."

5   It was about 30 feet long and weighed about 2 tons. Along its back were two rows of diamond-shaped plates. The plates were used for protection, along with the spikes on its tail.

6   A hiccup occurs when a part of your body called the diaphragm squeezes and jerks. The sound that is made comes from air vibrating your vocal cords.

7   There are 9,000 taste buds on the front, back, and edges of your tongue. They determine if food is bitter, sweet, sour, or salty.

What's the big idea?!

8   Braille is a code that can be read by touch. For each letter, number, or punctuation mark, one or more of six dots are raised. It was developed in France by Louis Braille in 1824.

9   Codes are used by the military to keep plans secret. Sometimes friends have fun using codes to write notes to one another.

10   The volcano on Mt. Vesuvius in Italy had suddenly erupted. Many hundreds of years later, the city was discovered buried beneath the dust and lava. It looked much as it did in A.D. 79.

11   One part is the source of electricity, such as a battery. Another part is an electric device, such as a lamp. These parts are linked by a conductor to form a loop. For example, wire might conduct electricity from a battery to a lightbulb and from the lightbulb back to the battery.

12   Electrons move or push each other from atom to atom. When an atom gains or loses electrons, it becomes electrically charged.

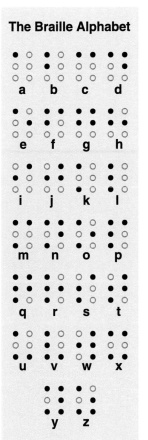

The Braille Alphabet

Answer Box

A	B	C	D	E	F
Scientists have defined this class as Insects.	An electric circuit has three main parts.	In A.D. 79, the city of Pompeii was completely buried.	Taste buds help you to taste food.	Electricity is made with energy from moving electrons.	The blue whale is the largest animal alive today.

G	H	I	J	K	L
The Stegosaurus was the largest of the plated dinosaurs.	Many people use secret codes.	The Tyranno-saurus Rex was probably the fiercest dinosaur.	The Triceratops was one of the largest horned dinosaurs.	Hiccups are a natural function of the body.	Blind people can "read" written words by using Braille.

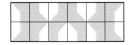

Objective: Identify the topic sentence (main idea) of a paragraph; practice comprehension and writing process skills.

29

Amounts and Order Matter

Read the recipe carefully. Pay attention to the ingredients you need and the order in which you add them.

 Charlie's Chunky Chocolate Chip Cookies

2 cups flour

1 teaspoon baking soda

1 teaspoon salt

1 cup softened butter

1 teaspoon vanilla

2 eggs

$\frac{3}{4}$ cup sugar

$\frac{3}{4}$ cup brown sugar

$\frac{1}{2}$ cup walnuts
(coarsely chopped in large chunks)

$1\frac{1}{2}$ cups semi-sweet chocolate chips

Preheat oven to 375 degrees. Combine flour, baking soda, and salt in a small mixing bowl. In a large mixing bowl, mix together butter, vanilla, eggs, and the sugars. Stir together the butter mixture and the flour mixture. Add the chocolate and walnuts. Scoop the dough into tablespoon-sized balls and place these on an ungreased cookie sheet. Bake for 10 minutes.

When you write your own recipes, remember to be specific. What might happen if you aren't?

Order the ingredients as you would add them to the *large* mixing bowl.

1 First, ▨

2 Second, ▨

3 Next, ▨

4 Then, ▨

5 After that, ▨

6 Finally, ▨

Answer these questions about the recipe.

7 Which ingredients should be combined first?

8 Which ingredient should be chopped?

9 When should you heat the oven?

10 How long should you bake the cookies?

11 How much dough is used for each cookie?

12 What ingredients are first mixed with the sugars?

Answer Box

A	B	C	D	E	F
walnuts	walnuts and chocolate	one tablespoon	eggs	10 minutes	the sugars
G	**H**	**I**	**J**	**K**	**L**
vanilla	butter, vanilla, and eggs	before you begin mixing	flour mixture	butter	flour, baking soda, and salt

Objective: Read and interpret directions in a recipe; practice comprehension and writing process skills.

31

At the Pet Store

Mr. Popper's Pet Store is a popular place to purchase a pet! Read each description. Find the pet that best matches the description.

1 Carrina bought an animal that would run and fetch.

2 Jacob's pet purrs through its whiskers.

3 Chen is a swimmer, so he purchased a pet that can swim.

4 Dusty had to buy a bridle and saddle to go with his animal.

5 Annie bought a hairy mammal. In spite of its name, it doesn't oink!

6 Dominic bought an animal that looks like a mouse with a long tail.

7 Joline's pet is a reptile that doesn't have legs.

8 David bought an animal that looks like an ordinary lizard, but it changes colors.

9 Charlotte's pet has feathers.

10 Richard bought a reptile that looks like a small dinosaur.

11 Maria's animal will hop around the yard!

12 Marco likes hide-and-seek, so he bought an animal that can hide in its shell.

Answer Box

A	B	C	D	E	F
rabbit	guinea pig	gerbil	cat	iguana	snake

G	H	I	J	K	L
bird	fish	turtle	chameleon	dog	horse

Objective: Use details to draw conclusions; practice comprehension skills.